T0114645

Fire in Paradise

Malthouse African Poetry

Fire in Paradise

Uzoechi Nwagbara

Department of Human Resource Management,
Greenwich School of Management, London, UK

Malthouse Press Limited

Lagos, Benin, Ibadan, Jos, Port-Harcourt, Zaria

© Uzoechi Nwagbara 2016
First Published 2016
ISBN 978-978-8422-54-9

Published by
Malthouse Press Limited
43 Onitana Street, Off Stadium Hotel Road
Off Western Avenue, Surulere, Lagos
E-mail: malthouse_press@yahoo.com
malthouselagos@gmail.com
Tel: +234-(0)802 600 3203

Dedication

To Fred –
the pelican bird lugging victuals in his pouch,
hedging us from hunger
exacerbated by the globalists!

To the other Fred –
father to the man:
The incendiary shell by SHELL
Threatens the future of your generation!
(With a united stand, your generation will win the green war!)

And to you all –
''penury patented people'' in the Niger delta,
Whose poverty pens a painful papyrus of privation!

Acknowledgements

I'm eternally grateful to God for making my "doodles" publishable! I am thankful to Professor Tanure Ojaide, a dream-maker (in my opinion) and the high-priest of African eco-criticism for making this possible. Professor Ojaide's handshake brought this publication to being; he showed me the way to Malthouse Press and I am amazed at their efforts to see *Fire in Paradise* hit the bookshelves; I say: much obliged!

I am indebted to my wife, Ngozi, who would "hibernate" taking the children away so that daddy could do his "business" – reading and writing! I'm sorely and surely bowled over at the depth of her love and sacrifice to me and the children. My thanks go to our "great boys": Fred, Jesse and King for strengthening my nerves to write more as they "disturb" daddy. Also, my gratitude goes to my mother, for instilling in us with papa the desire to question things: the harbinger of knowing. Thanks for germinating the seed! Finally, I'm grateful to my siblings particularly my great elder brothers: Dee Uche and Prof Onyinye Nwagbara, for shaping my intellectual quest; I'm also grateful to Ebbie, my kid brother, as well as our kid sisters: Udo and Uru.

Foreword

The title itself, *Fire in Paradise*, encases a basic paradox. Hell which is an antithesis of heaven is fire-laden hence the word hell-fire. Heaven or Paradise on the other hand is peaceful and tranquil, happy and satisfying hence the term heavenly bliss. Fire in the Niger Delta paradise has shattered the peace and tranquillity that marked that riverine paradise with its simple and contented citizens. But then deltas in the world mostly are problematic spaces, them being a blessed and cursed environment in a paradox of life and living. This is because of their difficult terrain and the wealth of crude oil and minerals hidden under the surface. Thus the Delta has always posed a problem of under-development world -wide. We cite the Mississippi delta in the United States of America. The basic question is what has ignited the raging fire in the paradise of the Niger Delta? What are its nature, size and form? What steps are taken for its containment? These are the issues Nwagbara's book of poems addresses.

Nwagbara's collection chronicles the odyssey of the people of Niger Delta and the nation of Nigeria by extension which spans the decades of the fifties till the present. This odyssey is still unfolding in a convoluting eddy. The first poem "Collegiate Hanging" introduces the poetic discourse in "medies res" with the hanging of the Ogoni 9. Their leader here named as NEK the messiah of the Delta, features the acronym in reverse order of Ken or Ken Saro-wiwa?:

> Executors perfected military skills
> To extinguish the mandarin of the nine,
> Whose end the gods had foreordained for a purpose:
> To heal our earth of this monstrous rape!

This rape of the region's crude oil resources started in 1956 with the discovery and exploration of crude oil. The Niger Delta is a placid place with a population of fishermen and farmers. Their aquatic domain provides them with their means of sustenance, their values and belief systems and the overall tranquil atmosphere of their life. As the saying goes, "Water no get enemy" But this domain, their paradise is to erupt with the fire of the discovery of crude oil in Oloibiri. With fire in the aquatic paradise, life changed dramatically .This oil boom in the nation's economy spelt doom for the land and people of Niger Delta. In the poem "It was Peace", the poet traces the Before and the After of life and the environment attendant on the discovery of crude oil:

> Then it was peace over the earth
> ----------------------
> Today our environment knows no peace,
> Our ecosystem knows no harmony,
> For sure, our land rather knows
> Blow-outs, flares, slicks, spillages, pollution (p.23.)

He continues this trope of environmental degradation in the poem "My Vanishing Space"(26) and details how the people have lost control of their domain and the resources therein. The notion of death dots most of the poems which emanates from despair and the hopelessness of the situation. The poet outlines in caustic terms, the sheer torment of living and presents death as a welcome release and alternative:

> If death could
> Make me a garment,
> I will dress up
> And come to it..........
> If death could,
> Let it form a hand
> Let it take me
> I need eternal rest.

The next movement in this poetic discourse is a sudden twist in the reaction of the people. From lament and passivity, the people resolve to fight back. The reasons are expressed in "Longest Poem I know":

> Environment extinct
> Education comatose
> Politics in rearguard action
> The masses on empty
> Government in deficit
> Corruption in surplus
> Ignorance on the mountain
> Morals in the valley. (p.15)

With this situation, we note in the memorable poem "When the Minorities are Hungry", that the die is cast and we indeed see that a hungry man is an angry man for the poem ends with these words:

> ....
> We don't eat dust, we survive,
> That's our nature
> That is at the tether's end:
> Men don't cry, they fight.

And that is precisely what the inhabitants of the Niger Delta did in life and in art. Violence marks the reaction of the youths in their various organizations. In "Men in Boots", the author etches the 1999/2000 brutal reaction of soldiers in Odi town in Bayelsa State to the violent restiveness of the youths in the area. The youths' resolve is seen in their affirmation of self:

> Till our dying day in the delta,
> A place we were placed by creation's choice,
> We reject to accept
> What they want us to be;
> We spurn their interpretation
> Of whom we are,
> We are who we truly are:
> We have got what oils the engines of the world,
> That's our individuality.
> Simple.   (p. 38.)

The delta youths resort to violence as a means of reclaiming their land, environment and oil wealth. The fight is contained in their domain where the drilling is done and the pollution occurs. Thus in the poem with the alliterative title "Shelling Shell & CO Ablaze", the youths launch attacks on oil installations of the foreign companies in the Delta and they really "Bomb Shell and cohorts ablaze"(p. 43.):

> Shell them ablaze for our environment sake
> Fight them to be green. (p.43)

Citing Ngugi Wa Thiong'o in "Physical Game (Escape Route 2)" Nwagbara sees physical violence as a means of change which purifies man. Of the three escape routes he posits in this collection, he endorses violence as a justifiable means to an end. He argues in this poem that "Passivity never chokes oppression but elongates the day of reckoning and holds man down..." There is a strong reference to the Theodore Adornian postulation that literature mediates social forms in society. Here Nwagbara views society with a social lens of the masses, the people denied their right to their possession and their labour. They suffer under the yoke of the elites, the bourgeois and eventually try to shake off this yoke through revolutionary means. Thus literature here is appreciated as a "weapon of mass struggle". (Mikics, p.175)

Nwagbara's collection is a political allegory of a nation in turmoil of self-realization, self acclaim and survival from the mitigating calamities that assail it. *Fire in Paradise* is reminiscent of the proto Miltonian title of *Paradise Lost* and the efforts of the people to regain their paradise. The poems toward the end of the collection show the tortuous efforts of the people at *Paradise Regained*. The fire in the Delta paradise has not been extinguished but the poet shows that the future of its attainment is bright and promising. Thus the poems end with hope.

The ceaseless anger and rumbles of the heart of a nation and a region are well portrayed in the caustic language of the poems. There is intense anger and bitterness channelled within and without and its attendant hopelessness and helplessness for lack of a solution. Dawn comes after the painful realization that there is no dependency outside of self: that salvation lies on self. It is to the credit of Niger Delta people that with rugged determination and revolutionary zeal, they rise to right the wrongs and to no longer stand and stare. Revolutionary tropes as blood, death, stagnation dot the poems and Nwagbara excels in his picturesque imagery depicting an environment under destruction and a people hideously traumatized.

Nwagbara's poetry underscores the nature of New Historicism and its postulate that History mediates Literature and lends more meaning and significance to it. Instances of historicity include the execution of the Ogoni 9, including Ken Saro-Wiwa, youth restiveness in the Niger Delta, the formation of militant groups and the Egbesu all of which define the region with violence. Included in the list is the government's quest for a political resolution to the problem in the Oputa Panel. In the final analysis it is the violence in the region that gave teeth to the people's agitation for government's support in the region's development. The Delta is regaining its paradise, Nwagbara writes in "Vernal Breeze":

> A fresh new breeze is blowing from all cusps
> An earth refreshed by peace is coming to stay
> Its inhabitants unfettered, unhitched..........
> We behold an era in retreat, bowing to the silent spring:
> ....
> Silent spring is raining on the land
> ....
> Brooks are springing to quench our thirst
> Anew order is sojourning to dwell among us...(p.55)

Nwagbara in a Marxist mode, portrays that such violence has its redeeming feature. It forces the notice of government seen in such ameliorating details as education, skills acquisition, employment opportunities that foster youth development and empowerment. This indeed is Literature as Revolution which succeeds in its anger and immediacy. It is daring but result-oriented and the important factor is that it succeeds even in its historicity. It is anticipated that Nwagbara will produce a sequel to this collection to show the regained paradise in the Niger Delta.

Helen Chukwuma, PhD
Professor of English, Department of English and Modern Foreign Languages, Jackson State University, Jackson. Mississippi. USA.

Preface

Fire in Paradise is a collection of poems refracting a grisly environment of virulent socio-economic, political and cultural overlap, where national identity and imperialist ethos collide headlong. The collection refracts a cavalcade of broken humanity, as well as their flora and fauna torpedoed by the powerful in the Niger Delta and Nigeria by extension. The written word in this collection takes us on a tramp of the Niger Delta, a theatre of horror – a place of smoke and mirrors for the masses, who are "the wretched of the earth", to use Fanonian locution.

The poems sing from the same songbook; their texture and timber coalesce to add zest to the title: *Fire in Paradise* – a dead ringer of Ken Saro-Wiwa's Ogoniland, a once-upon-a-time paradise turned into a wasteland. A verse in the collection, "Longest Poem (I Know)", silhouettes this dreary backwater:

> Environment extinct
> Ecology comatose
> Politics in rearguard action...

Same act, different scripts for other poems in the collection. In "Vanishing Space", a similar perspective is knelled: "of all my worries, the most, is my vanishing space..." The refrain of destroyed human condition, environmental pollution and ecological dissonance percolate the entire collection: "Oil of Tears", "When the Earth Cries" and others verses offer similar distillation. In sum, *Fire in Paradise* touches off our collective consciousness towards understanding the Niger Delta hangs in the balance.

However, there are verses that offer a flicker of hope mediated by imagery of resistance and tropes of stubborn hope; they include among others "Intimations of Grit" and "I Believe", whose sinews soothe our bruises. This versification goes on to engraft if we believe in the magic of "sweat" – by not limited by the numbing and searing space in the Niger Delta – we can change our environment as well as transform Nigeria.

Table of Contents

Collegiate Hanging

Their execution, hanging
Calls forth a dance,
We're learning its thorny choreography –
A monstrosity of a kind,
An act with impunity,
Forever, a living memory, although past!

As they execute them, their innocent cries
At this gory moment
Could not blunt the edge of the hangmen's howling sin…
No interpretation needed:
They have touched the earth the most.
Their last words could not roll back their credo!
Today we celebrate their will to die,
A gaping imprints on the sands of time:
That's what they left on the annals of history,
A memory, silhouetting a tonic –
Our children's children will read it,
With angst, the earth will remember it!

During the execution, Nek, the messiah of the delta
Rustled his last words:
Supposedly, a measured, sobering rendition
To quench their hunger for blood;
But their proviso negated his emotive pills;
Their agenda chased away his corona –
This unassailably starred them in the face.

The execution
Unearths musical chairs –
Executors perfected military skills
To extinguish the mandarin of the nine,
Whose end the gods had foreordained for a purpose:

To heal our earth of this monstrous rape!
His pleaded grace
The gods ignored for a road show:
To tell it on the mountain for the world to know!
The execution
Acts a collegial script;
We're grappling with its dramatic upshot.
How can a regimen affront history?
This will forever be a memory aid
For our coming children
To re-write the script
And act it out!

Elegy For Nek, The Warrior

Your angst was insufferable -
You rather squeaked through victory
With grace under pressure,
Your abiding lodestar -
For beyond the incandescence of command and obey;
Beyond the blather of ethnicity, the blaze of conceit;
Across the jarring blares, the cackling laughter of derision -
Beyond the asphyxiating afterglow of 'revenue sharing
    formula',
That ensconces the ghoulish spell of incarceration - the
    numbing fear of dying,
You witnessed the glint in history's eyes –
Of hope, conquest and triumph
Lying groggily at the portal of time.

From all corners of our mind,
You etched the evergreen memorabilia:
Of warrior's paraphernalia –
All lighting up our minds, path, cause.
After you disappeared,
We still trail the corona over your head, our rider
To get to the ballpark of the history you foresaw with your sixth
    sense.
With the corona,
You blazoned a flambeau,
Illuminating the landscape within
After you're gone.
With your words of immortality,
You mounted a bust for yourself, overlooking your tombstone,
All in our hearts.
We see this tomb each day –
In our hearts, your tomb is marked;
Not unmarked as the vampires thought!

3

With your deeds,
You spoke through the deafening noise,
And we heard clearly your clarion call:
We will always be goaded by its tonic.
With your unwavering mind,
You opened the postern,
Which we walk through
To embrace our destiny –
(After the predators shut the portal against us):
Not the one in the catacombs of the disfigured earth.
With your grit,
You added another page
To the history of Ogoniland.

Your flirtation with the arts
Has opened the portal for you in the pantheon of the literati;
Your seasoned vocal pontification –
Often labelled demagoguery as their alibi for evil,
Has made you a mast for the global ship
Carrying legions of humanity to a "free world".
Your vision for the Niger delta,
Has left imprints on the sands of environmental conservation -
Our ancestors dance in their grave for your credo:
Their waists full of pain
As they danced to the bliss
Your lighted mind brought to our land.

Wreckages of the Gulf

Memories undaunted by the present charade
Are what those periods are:
They're memories cooked with
The concoctions of a coven's cuisine;
These times grind our collective thoughts
On the anvil of misery;
These times, write the algebra of the unsolvable in the minds of
the visited.

In the gulf,
We found bones, skulls, pieces of flesh,
hanging loose from their places;
They're anonymous,
'cause their owners have be gone a journey,
Leaving them behind.
That gulf, is a place for the "cursed" blessed.

In our gulf,
The hall of famers of infamy,
Find abode in the land of skulls,
'cause the owners of the once-upon-a-time peaceful abode,
Had set out at midnight
To return no more
For their new home sustains their crunch.

Memories unhindered by road show,
Are what the times are,
That try men's souls,
A period when our body trembles;
The habitat is set into unusual frenzy
By the activities of the men of loot.

In that gulf, cooking utensils, charred bodies, broken glasses,
cinders…
All clutter to point at where we were coming from:
The trees danced to the serenading songs of birds in that space;
It was an ocean of great deafening silence,
Hidden from the reach of predators!

Behind The Backcloth

The picture cannot show:
No truth, no gcnuinc report:
But charade, endless misinformation,
All phony in a million way.
New taffeta, same place, disparate happenstance –
Our eyes, ears, noses
See, hear and smell
This gory plain.

Behind the stage,
Mankind means nothing to the hatchet men,
The riders whose eyes know no remorse;
They're carriers of putrid wishes, potent evil;
They weave, execute charges,
Propagating "operation shoot at sight".
Once this operation is weaved,
They run amok to execute the innocents,
Whose fate hangs in the balance:
Their fate oscillates
between the lyric of these hangmen and the prayers of the
people.

Behind the taffeta,
A brigandage is set in motion.
No one to refute the charges;
What a kangaroo set-up?
Behind, there's an avatar of the master's mission:
To level the unconverted,
And to spare the proselytised candidates
for their petro-dollar kingdom!
The stubborn can't be spared behind this backcloth!

Behind the page,
Leads a million of pages,
Dancing to the song of infamous machination,
Strewn with avalanche of incarcerations, allegations,
assassinations
Finding detonation in the well-being of the plebeians.

Behind the closed door,
Brews credo of Hitler's Gestapo policing;
Humans caught for the master's falconry,
Whose song lyricises a nation with power blocs
Crying for attention, milked dry by environmental
haemorrhage.

Behind the iron curtain,
Hides chthonic twirls of pipes
Scattered on the seafronts, on beaches, in bushes, on our roads
In a form that leaves the bootlegged ghouls in stitches.
As their date with our "representatives" is kept!

The message does not show;
No indication, no reliable clue:
But a smokescreen of disservice,
All sham in an unusual manner.
The same Niger Delta, the same place, but different act –
Our hairs stood up as we saw where men are buried:
Shallow graves.
No depth, 'cause the living were in a hurry;
They don't want to follow the dead.

Behind the story told about this Niger Delta,
harbours pieces of travesty garnished with the reporting.
The Niger Delta saga is better told by them;
Not their newsmen,
Who blow hot and cold with the same measure of breath.
The Niger Delta is poetry in motion,

It's about becoming an apocalypse:
The theatres follow a shadow of
BETRAYAL.

Foursquare Hope

1.
Our eyes have seen minds consumed by hopelessness:
Fog lies in wait, thorns have sprung in all places.
Having been mauled by marketplace of men's activities,
The pine trees are no more abodes for the storks.
The birds can't make their nests, the conies stolen from the
crags;
The craws are breakneck, furious for food -
The fodders have begun a journey, their whereabouts
indeterminate, disconcerting.
We feel human traffic - all coming for the hay;
Space grazed, clawed.
The sun ignorant of time to go down; moon unable to mark off
the seasons…
The pawing of nature running this riot;
Aquatics storm-tossed, dead creatures from the seas swarm our
shorelines.
We touch faces shorn of reason to live;
The eyes of the earth within,
Look like a valley in dire straits for repose.

2.
Our concerted grit stilled the storm,
Which like clouds and whirlwind, did not call forth rain.
With ironclad mind, we shook-out our planet, story…
The dengue of the tropic was at bay,
All because we farmed hope on that muddying, grating
landscape,
That killjoy of the innocents.

3.
We have wrestled with men in rearguard action:
For more arsenals, more arrows in their quiver, and more fire
in their guns...
Fear has inhabited our minds, from the quadrangle of our
imagination.
The president proclaims our end,
Their craftsmen forge it,
Their goldsmiths overlay their marching order with spikes.
Like the spread of the sky, our dark days are there for everyman
to see.
Water fountains broken; cisterns made for us -
Eyesight is failing from famine; panting jackals are what our
donkeys have become.
Our days of hurricane are graphed with flint point,
They're underwritten by our bequest they carted.
From the crest of the mountains and the nadir of the valleys,
our parched, withered earth...
Smells of fumes, gases, hunger - wrought upon us by these
kings.

4.
In the desert of hope, there comes oasis of directed steps:
Within this cosmos, ashes trade places with cedars.
What other signs do we desire to know?
The locusts are in retreat.
Theirs are pages from the scorching sun -
...Book of death, it's about
Holding out strong in the face of life-threatening situation.
They're gone to never return!

Longest Poem (I Know)

Environment extinct
Education comatose
Politics in rearguard action
The masses on empty
Government in deficit
Corruption in surplus
Ignorance on the mountain
Morals in the valley

Inogo, The Fallen City

See Inogo
Where nobody recognises grey hair
See Inogo
Where people spit at those whose backs are bent with age.
Look at Inogo
Where man means nothing to man
Follow me to this space
Where dog eats dog
Man's stomach matters more than human essence
In this land
The king is the only mountain
Masquerading as the avatar
Whose breath gives life
And takes it away as he pleases
The people are mere molehill

In Inogo
We must pick through a minefield
Before the 'area boys' assassinate or even steal us
We must bow and scrape
Else the king's men will keep us high and dry
Follow me to Inogo
Where everybody is a drudge
Only the king's men are the blue-collared
Egbesu Boys opportunists, Bakassi Boys comrades

In Inogo
No body tills the land nor has a book in their hands
Expect politics, militancy, vandalism
The shrines are packed with men
Who want to be the next king
Ballooning the pockets of high priests
With Inogo's money

13

In Inogo
Values have gone up in smoke
Charred, mutilated limbs left
Face gnarled, legs ripped apart
Eyes plucked out
Not in contact with our ancestral lore
It's left helplessly gnashing its teeth
Even as they're dead

When The Earth Cries...

When the earth cries
We see the harrowing gulf
Between North and South;
We witness the jarring nexus
Between hope and fear.

When the earth cries
An uncanny iron-curtain is unveiled,
The divide between the rich and the poor
Is unveiled;
We come to grips with a quirk:
Of blazing panoply of dysfunction,
Especially of lives, earth sitting on fire.

When the earth cries
A kaleidoscope of grotesque toga is removed –
The works of warlords are uncovered;
We see through the smokescreen: fawning compatriots –
Of townsmen on a mission for their own agenda:
Personality cult, their fetish,
Cowardice, their catechism,
Their belly, their religion.

When the earth cries
We see bloodless quislings,
Parading as part of us;
We see a cavalcade of the innocents –
We know having a dog born in a stable does not make it a
horse.

15

When the earth cries
We bleed,
They laugh;
We burn,
They sizzle.

When the earth cries
The cinders hidden in the mountainous heap of ashes
Welcome us to the crunch of the boulder, rocks, rivers, lakes,
forests;
As the earth cries,
I hear the sound of their prodigal dealings
Echoing eyes expectant of bread,
Hands tired of waiting for manna,
Tongues languid as they wait to quench thirst in the sun,
Feet numb from endless standing.

When the earth cries
Multitudes of hangmen descend on the innocents
With ravenous hunger for blood,
The crimson fluid that pacifies their masters,
Who watch them mutilate our lean, tremulous world
Like implacable avengers.
Witnessing our earth bleed,
We're frozen on the inside, but holding out brave faces
So that the killers may retreat.
Not even our make-believe bravery could force them to retreat:
For blood must be on their hands
For their masters' glee…

Memory and Reality

Rivers of blood flow through the delta;
Innocent lives slaughtered on the altar of racial hate
Precipitate the oceanic flow.
Seas of heads gaze hopelessly
To recognise their own dead –
Those dead in endless war for endless peace search.
Makeshift coffins draped with flags they died for -
The reason for the flag made comatose by their agenda.
Temporary this must be
For we are no more the innocents they knew:
Yes we may be guiltless, but we are not naïve;
The Spirit of the times has quickened our knowledge…
We know the value of what is under our feet from creation.
Our innocents have been forcefully taken away
From our very eyes in a hurry,
Their cries have met heaven –
This meeting will be complete
When we name the day:
When we shall carry war to all doorsteps,
Asking for a return of our innocents, bequests.

Oceans of tears flow through our land,
Since the great discovery: Olobiri I curse you for opening up!
Their plan mediated by hegemony theory,
Sustaining volcanic flow of blood.
Our 'men of honour,'
corrupted by their belated activities -
They feather the nests of the overlords;
They have rendered our delta near barren for our crops, trees,
aquatics…
We unwittingly welcome them as collaborators
To build our space,

Which is in dire straits for growth.
Now, we know their true colour:
They kill and bury for good!
At the dead of the night,
Our blameless blood,
Will stir them in the face,
Lacerating their ballooned bellies -
Emptying the contents on our delta
For our vegetation needs them to blossom once again!

Oil of Tears

They're the rulers
Of this space of flesh-eating vermin
And this valley of bones,
Poisoned by the master's fiat.

They're the masters
Of the harlequin stage management,
This mountain of squalor,
Enfeebled for their looting.

They're taking the oil:
The staccato of bullets
Shooting from all imaginable locus
Acts the script.
Why the land red?
The grass brown?
The water red?

The oil:
Nature's bequest;
The oil of tears
Flowing with red-hot ferocity;
It runs through their mega-long pipes
Under our own feet
To wherever they want –
It goes in a hurry
Leaving us in TEARS!

Let Me Die

1.
Let me die,
Be dead,
leave this polluted universe for what
It has become -
Rather than drown the godhead in me
in the oil, waters of their vice-grip torture.

Each passing season chimes
in the footsteps of a déjà vu;
and I, entrapped in tears.

2.
Let me die,
be gone,
say goodbye to this vestigial space,
for it will not bring rest
to my soul;
my earth has evaporated.

Each day roars
like a roaring lion;
and I, ensnared in misery.
Let me die,
let me go away,
let me leave this empty space.

A Visit To The Crypt

We went to places
Where men have died,
We sweated and looked for the faces
Of those for whom we have lamented, cried, groaned…
Their body parts have disappeared into the air,
Their spirits have begun a journey
Somewhere not defined, clear, known -
Somewhere beyond death.
Where on earth does grief go?
What does it show?
Where does it sit?
On ashen lips? (maybe)
The flowers are gone,
The cries are over,
The groaning is over,
The earth is still now…
But the talk will not redeem us
For we're deadened by this 'visit';
Our spirit is on the ice for this terror,
For we may not be the same again.
A priest sent from Abuja
Can do no magic!

It Was Peace

Then it was peace over the earth –
In the air there was stillness;
In the sea there was rest;
On the shore we played about.

Today our hearts know no peace;
Today our earth knows no joy;
Today our shores know no quiet.

Today beckons whirlwind,
Today approaches with cyclone,
Today comes like lightning.

Then it was festivities over the land –
In the markets, at the beaches, on the shores;
At our homes we declared feasts;
In the churches we prayed away our pains.

Today our environment knows no peace,
Our ecosystem knows no harmony,
For sure, our land rather knows
Blow-outs, flares, slicks, spillages, pollution.

Today there is no song in our hearts,
Today no merry-making
For we are sad for the gnarled earth!

Death Labourers

They marched on strongly
on our shorcs,
They rode unabatedly
on our farmlands,
They talked magisterially
at our oil wells, village squares,
They wore their rigger boots, hard hats, vests, gloves, goggles
They are heavenly protected
against our will, mind, sanction!

They're coming
with a large army, whose face knows no remorse;
An army strengthened
by the chief's fiat;
An army reinforced
by the president's choice;
An army empowered
by mortgaged conscience.

This army is riding rough shod
on our psyche, collective will;
This army, a product of state arrangement lacks morality;
This army, a partner
in crime against popular opinion is marching on.

But the gates of popular choice will stop it!
It's machete wielding powers
Through the gun-trotting macho
Cannot save ruins lying
in wait for these men in boots!

The Vanished Garden

They stood –
drop-dead still –
Listening to the murmuring;
In the gardens, trees rustled captivatingly,
Casting rippled shades across the landscape.
The breeze sets pendulous trees and flowers nodding, dancing:
All swaying in joyous rhythm!

Suddenly, the garden was 'visited':
Its flora mangled.
Its fauna wasted.
Those left behind could not find the 'dancing garden';
It was lost to a flash of decision:
There was smoke,
Thick smoke, forming ripples in the air;
The garden was under rubbles!

The whirring smoke had oscillated to the people;
The people are not caged by the thinking of dying,
They have resolved to get their 'dancing garden'!

My Vanishing Space

Of all my worries, the most, is my vanishing space;
Not the fate of the newly born,
Not the way of the eagles in the sky,
Not the fate of the crippled,
Not the way of the blind, or the fate of an orphan.
But to know ashes are on my lips while I live,
Puts me in another space before I know it!

Of all my headaches, the most, is my vanishing space;
Not the unending pains of Smithian triad,
Not the colour of Abuja politics,
Not the way of the village chiefs, our 'representatives', ethnic
    militias…
Not the mandate of 'area boys', or the politics of war-
    mongering.
But to reckon that our region is in neglect while we draw
    breath,
Takes our breath away before we know it!

If Death Could, Let It...

If death could
Build a stairway,
I will walk up to it
And have a rest.

If death could
Make me a garment,
I will dress up
And come to it.

If death could
Form a river,
I will swim against these chains
And meet it.

The sanctuary of death
Is the key to unlock
My toil and sweat
Brought upon me by man's design.
The fortress of death
Will see me through
My wreck and drain.

If death could,
Let it spare me a space
In its multitude of abodes
For I want to come home.

If death could,
Let it form a hand:
Let it take me,
I need eternal rest.

Find Us A Shelter...

Strewn with thick flames,
Our earth lost good inhalation;
Cluttered with wreckage of flaring,
Our land lost its vegetation;
Threaded with plunder and killing,
Our children lost their ancestors.

Find us a place to dwell
For here is consumed,
Find us a shelter to hide
For we are in sweltering sun,
Find us a land to farm
For here is barren.

Shelter us from fear
Nuanced with bloodletting, tainted with morbidity;
Shelter us from war
Tempered with shooting, topped with hate;
Shelter us from politics
Garnished with hate, seasoned with terror –
Find us a shelter in which
We could hide away from rain.

Bitter Than Death

Bitter than death
This way must be –
Whichever the hue of the bell that tolls,
For the happenstance has taken our lions, bests, bequest…

Bitter than death
This moment must prove -
Whichever direction the wind blows,
For the drilling has eclipsed our sun…

Bitter than being in the grave
This season is -
Whichever thing that happens,
For the season has taken our all into thralldom…

Bitter than death
This meeting must be –
Wherever we meet,
For this meeting reminds us our liquidation…!

When The Minorities Are Hungry

1.
When men are hungry they fight,
When men are hungry they cry,
When men are hungry they make a noise,
When men are thirsty they drink water,
When men are dirty they bathe.

When men are pushed to the wall they rebound,
When they are seized, they clamour for freedom,
When they are plundered, they ask why…
To regain their place, bequest, harvest.

2.
When men fight, their lands are made whole,
When they push down barriers, nothing limits them,
When they ask question, they find answers,
When they level the mountains, they see beyond the horizons,
When they knock, doors are open.

When men sit back and watch tyranny, they're helmed in,
When the theatre is for the weak, no actual drama happens,
When they allow our oil to be ferried to another land,
we don't eat dust, we survive,
that's our nature
that is at the tether's end:
Men don't cry, they fight.

On Grief and Grieving

We sat on wooden benches,
Clad in rags,
Looking scruffy, ashes on our heads,
Our feet had no shoes,
For we can't buy them;
We knew nothing but cry.
Our bellies aching from lack of food;
Our eyes have formed gullies, our hairs dishevelled,
Our minds imprisoned by their shooting.
We're at last made strangers in our own land
By the power of command and obey -
Our souls have bowed to this unconscionable power;
We are coming to the end of the road.

We sat on muddy ground,
Adorned in regalia,
Hoping confidently in the power of the shrine:
Our hands had no knives, bucklers, bludgeons, rapiers
For we can't buy any after the raid on our environment;
We knew nothing but hoping on the 'freeing' powers of the
    gods.
Our chests gone flat from terror,
Our bibles are lost to raid, heist…
Our spirit is caged by their fire-balling armies.
The priest is eaten up by the fear that they will maim him.
Who shall save our land from this sacrilege?
The good men are "dead";
We're at the crossroads;
We're in grief.

The Sorrow Garden

1

I walked through a dark, sequestered garden,
The trees turned into vapour,
The soil barren from perennial sapping.
When I looked back,
I saw dead people walking towards me:
They did not have legs
But they walked,
Only bright pair of eyes
Showing me the way to get out of the ghosted garden.
The sorrow garden was a ghost town,
Looking like a ghost of its former self;
Its shrubs are gnarled from blow-outs, its fruits mangled as the gases are taken.
As I turned around,
I was greeted by the walking dead,
Who told me to tell the living to put our world in order.
These spirits did not have hands, but they showed me the damages done to our space.
They only had a voice that calibrated the impending dangers of fence-sitting.

2

The evergreens used to dance to the undulating breeze of floral wholesomeness:
It's now a peneplain;
A child of circumstance, whose fate lay in the hands of jackboots;
As I walked through this once-upon-a-time beauty,
There was a mental fixation on the splendour of nature,
The masterstroke of creation
that could only be quantified by the ever presence of order.

31

Symmetry was at the heart of its chemistry, art and beauty meet at its essence;
The sorrow garden was a mirror that showed the nature of God;
We could see Him in the mirror of nature -
Perfection was his other name.
The sorrow garden has evaporated into the universe of exploration.
Years of hitting hard on the space has caved in on us all!
Accounting for this abysmal wind of change,
Is the logic for the carnage, war, ethnic cleansing…
The sorrow garden, throws up the mantra of gas chamber on our lips,
It brings the horrors of Odi saga to our doorsteps,
It points a flambeau to the Ogoni savagery,
The sorrow garden is a signpost to Umuechem.
The sorrow garden is a bull's eye of sacrilege.
This garden, a place of skulls - 'ethnic Golgotha'.

Men in Boots

Who are these men
That maim, loot, kill, pollute
Without blinking,
Rather with impunity?

Who are these people
Who freeze our land,
Bulldoze our inheritance
And march to the songs of war?

Who are these
Who turn our world upside down
And remind us of Gestapo blues,
And clutter our land with skulls and bones?
Where on earth
Are they from
That don't listen
To reason, justice, equity?

These men's hearts know no law;
Their noses smell no justice;
Their ears hear no pity;
Their eyes see no good.

They are from the land called 'Kilidem',
That place that knows no 'brother'
Except partners in crime.

2
Who are they
That make us cringe
At their bestiality?
Who are these scions that make us weep
In the day of dancing?
They give us weeping when we ask for dancing.
Who are they that siphon our oil to their cohorts
As other worlds bring booties home
To their own people?
They must be beasts of no nations,
Spoiled by the spoils of office,
That they know no umbilical affiliation.
Who are these uniform men that kill and bury
In the time of peace
Instead of pontificating healing?
They must be from the 'ethnic-minded tribe',
Who want nothing but the size of their stomach,
Which enlarges as our earth burns.
They offer dirge in a time of paean.

When I Remember It (I Cringe)

My heart aches when I think of it,
My flesh yellows as I think of it;
I cringe to think of this mass killing.

I have got to go on
Living with the hellish memory of this day

My heart flutters as I sojourn through this dreary landscape;
My being fritters when I make this arcane mentally punishing
transit;
I squirm as the thoughts grip me.

I have got to go on
Living with the harrowing thoughts of this killing

When I remember how men were reduced to pieces of meat;
How they're being taken to the abattoir for slaughter,
I wish I could upturn the landscape.

I have got to go on
Living with the apocalyptic feelings of that day

Something About Them

Something reminds me of them,
They have come to uproot us,
They have come to scatter us,
They have come to put us down.

One thing tells me about them,
They're our enemies,
They're the region's undoing -
They're our bane.

Something that shows their mind
Is their plan of attack,
Their long sojourn
To take our only worth.

There's something wrong with the way they look…
Value-free assessment, would put us into their hands.
Their panoply of "representatives" would make us deadweight
In this marketplace!

There is something about them,
That can't be smeared with retribution and reconciliation;
I can see through their ruse of humanitarian gesture,
Which serves as iron curtain to keep us down.

Something acts up their orchestration of attack,
Even when it's meddled with hypocrisy.
There's a thing about them,
No matter how they involve us in the business of peace –
this time with Father Kooka!

Smooth Operators

With razor-sharp talks
They have our leaders confused
To take our worth
In the name of negotiation

With sabre-rattling operation
They have our oil dug endlessly
To further impoverish us
In the name of tapping natural resources

With ironclad will
They hammer while the iron is red-hot
To melt away our oneness
So as to scatter us

With Janus-faced demeanour
They put on us a strait-jacket of political apathy
So we grope in political wilderness
While they loot us

With mountain of promises to build bridges where puddles
reign
They 'kwashiorkored' our collective will to build
Making us idlers in our own land
To further hold sway in the comity of nations

With poker-faced gawk
They couldn't offer explanation
For the heist
They've done to our Mother Earth

All We Want Is Life (Not Death)

Out of the wreckages,
Out of the dust,
Out of the ruins,
A new force will emerge
To repossess our earth
From the hands of the scoundrels.

Out of the tears,
Out of the blood,
Out of the sweat,
We're the ones left behind
To end in the dark
Or shine like life.

Out of the thunder dome,
Out of clatter of arms,
Out of the war,
We don't need another warrior;
All we want is life beyond the mountain heap of ashes.

Out of the side bars,
Out of the heap of unfiltered information,
Out of the grape vine,
A strong voice will rise to offer education
In this time of misinformation.

Out of the spillages,
Out of the pollutions,
Out of the devastations,
We see an earth afar
Coming down to dwell among us in peace:
Out of the fog,
Comes a bright season!

The Cynics

Till our dying day in the delta,
A place we were placed by creation's choice,
We reject to accept
What they want us to be;
We spurn their interpretation
Of whom we are;
We are who we truly are:
We have got what oils the engines of the world,
That's our individuality.
Simple.

We may be chased to the fringe,
Reeking there is something about us,
We surely belong to the centre –
Not of Nigeria alone –
But of the universe!
We reject their education:
They can't tell us better than we can tell ourselves,
We know who we are.
Simple.

We doubt their mental picture of us,
We are much bigger than that image.
Countrymen,
Think outside the box
For we are more than what they say.
There's more behind speech –
Full of flannel!
Simple.

We refute their report,
It will be turkeys –
No commercial success, landmark…
For it's phony.
Unless we doubt their propaganda,
There will be more deaths on our plain.
Simple.

Burial Mound

1.
On the mound our bodies are placed
For the appeasement sacrifice,
The pyres are ever ready
For the burning;
We're ready made combustibles for this rite of passage:
A fitting drama for the sustenance of the upper class.
The mound smells of generation punished
By their endowments,
An unfortunate species
Made prostrate by what it did not bargain;
Overly *victimised*,
Routinely *marginalised*,
Constitutionally *segregated*.

2.
On the mound
Vultures perch, some hover around us
Basking in the spirit of their usual delicacy;
Some food for their bellies, after all –
Our bodies are made for this meeting of vultures;
What a wheel of change for the poor of the earth?
The mound
Takes our nose through the squalor of misrepresentation:
A caricature of democracy,
An unholy alliance in the rainbow of ethnicities,
Made unrepresented by what is freely bestowed to it.
What an ill-fated region,
Perennially siphoned,
Judicially silenced,
Religiously targeted.

3.
On this burial mound
Our conscience is plumbed,
For "valuation",
The perks are ever present for this mortgaging.
On this mound,
Our ashes are collected
For their urns;
Their agents are handy
For this task.
On this mound,
We are charged with culture conflict,
Nay, regional attrition -
The prebendals, corporatists,
Positioned for this identity loss.

Intimations of Grit

Yield no more to brute force
Or we're arraigned as heretics.
By kowtowing to fallen doctrines,
We will be sentenced for 'rebellion.'
Never bow to hijacked authority
Before we're accused of apostasy.
Thread the part of self-professing godhead,
Else, the eye of the earth shall
Historically label us lily-livered.
By standing up for your creed in the oceans of heads,
We will be counted.
As we fill the craters of injustice with loads of right;
The Niger Delta shall never be their stamping ground again.
Standing unapologetically in the gaping hiatus of their deeds,
Our earth shall go asleep -
For it has known insomnia since Nembe Oloibiri discovery.
Let our lips mouth fire towards all corners
For our time has come, like a thief.
Flat chests can't push down these Jericho walls;
Only the clutters on our streets can reveal
That we're colliding headlong with these wrongs.
Their putrid corpses, that make the vultures swarm,
Can only forgive our humourlessly congenital, pathological
inertia…
We shall allow our hands shoot the guns,
Not our mouths, flannel -
For we will be HELD DOWN by it all these times;
By replacing verbal fight with the physical,
The torrential rain of reason, bodily harm
Will come down on us!
On their deaf ears.
A little dose of war frees our earth,

43

Than the ineffectuality of dialogue…
Too much dialogue is not good for our aching bodies.
Let us stop them before they stop us;
Let us stop these chemicals, toxic wastes, before they say:
"Good riddance" to us!

Spatial Fight

1.
Delta people whose space is besiegcd, marooncd
Are in a special fight;
The neglected whose soil is disabled
Fight a spatial fight.
A grain of falsehood
Has decimated them;
A seed of false nationhood,
Has dwarfed them...

2.
As they launch their sortie,
They run on empty –
A sating, choking fumes creep from the
Crevices;
Hungry faces crawl out from the
...Attacks, devices...

A Requiem For Our Lores

May you rest uneasy
Until your killers find death themselves…
Our social glue, the unseen that was obeyed,
May your murderers shake hands with death,
For you always communed with our forefathers -
Pontificating: pointing the flambeau for them
Towards good or bad.

May your tears spring from the tomb
Drown them and their offspring,
Who might come to put a nail into your coffin.
Let your fetid, putrid smell choke their lungs…
That they may die with thee.
May the coldness of grave remove sleep, warmth…
From your eyes,
From your heart.

Punch their paunches - evidence of their heist -
Let the innards go under the ground,
To bring some of you back (that was taken).
You, who stood brief for us,
When we had no foodstuffs
To barter their "hay" -
You - like the pillars of the tablets of our hearts,
That always read out the riot act for us,
Whenever we transgressed.

May you never rest
Until they come unto you - gnashing their teeth.
You, the silent avenger .
Come in the dead of the night to take them.
Poke their eyes,
That the waters from them…
May refill our fountain of life -
Our lost earth -
…Part of you, at least!

Shelling Shell & Co. Ablaze

('My nativity gives immortal pain
Masked in barrels of oil').
--- *Tanure Ojaide*

Gone is the age of palaver,
It's disappeared from the confines of our reach;
Far gone is the period of quibble,
Located within the quadrangle of cemetery!
Satire has no relevance in this epoch,
Only earth-shattering mines
Hidden under their feet could keep them away.
Roundtable is in the coffin
Long dead, but not buried:
No broth, no water, no leaves for our stomach –
All gone to be with our forefathers, resting forever!
Our lands cry for green;
They're given red, brown.

Waste no time before they shoot you;
Spare none, for they will soon take advantage;
Don't look back before your conviction is neutralised.
Fill their empty faces with horrors,
Feed them with gunfire, shells, bombs…
That's the only language they hear –
Deaf bodies in search of who to immobilise.
Don't miss any shooting in this war
That's the way out.
Let Shell and others know:
We're poised to shell them ablaze.

Shell them with incendiary shell…
Let all corners receive pieces of their flesh;
Raise the bar, no mercy –
For they have come to end us!
Our lands are running empty of our largess;
Do the shelling before we all go down.
Aim like an archer
When you shell men of iniquity.
Leaving them unhurt,
Will leave us battered!
Dismantle their structures when you shell -
Else, they WILL spring back,
Like coiled snake in a mission to have a rat for lunch!

Bomb Shell and their cohorts ablaze,
Their double speak is mere antics –
Their perks are mere pittance to what they've taken:
That's the only whack they incur.
Never in this field of battle,
Shall we engage in talk
Shell them ablaze
Let the four corners of the earth know
We have done it,
Else we're pliable.
Execute them to keep our land environmentally friendly;
Shell them ablaze for our environment's sake;
Fight them to be green!

Abuja: The Bugbear

You speak fire from your mouth.
What comes from your eyes is violence.
From your nose comes bugaboo.
Communities freeze when you sneeze.
Your tongue tastes death.
Your hands rock our world –
Frightening the hell out of us.
Your breath stinks to heaven.
Your ear solicits news of new massacres.
Your mammoth legs crush our earth.
Your thick skin knows no pain
Rather insensate.
Our egrets have varnished for your credo.
Our eiderdown is on the run to the metropole for your whims.
The earth is our witness:
The cluttered seas, awash with flotsam and jetsam are our
exonerator.
You stage clambakes from the fruits of our seas, land…
You clambered our earth for slick substance.
Your ruse greases the palm of ethnic militias.
Your centre, is your sinew,
…From that cusp, you draw all unto yourself.
Beauty by design, not by nature –
But by politics.
Communities form cyst at your heart
To palaver their ruin.
Abuja, the trouble with us!
You're a place of artificial assemblage:
What gives you life is our lifelessness.
You have no blood,
But you're always in the pink;
While we're in red!

You stay at home to know what happens around the nation,
You're omniscient indeed!
FCT -
Familiar criminal in town.
You're habitually on the prowl
Looking for preys –
Innocents of the earth.
People know you're a child of design and circumstance!
Trouble us less before we lose our temper.
Abuja, centre of smoke and mirrors.

Mind Game (Escape Route One)

('The only weapon in the hands of the oppressed,
is the mind of the oppressor'.)
--- *Steve Biko.*

The
Only
Channel
Of
Escape
Is
Our
Mind
That
Inconsequential
which
Matters
 Is
The
Only
 Way
Out
Of
This
Terrorising
Spell
It
May
Be
Long
To
Get
Out
Of
The

Impasse
But
I
Think
It's
The
Best
Option
It
May
Seem
Tortuous
But
That's
The
Healer
Of
Our
Unjustly
Inflicted
Wounds
Set
On
Us
By
The
Bad
Men
Of
The
Land
Our
Joy
Now
Our

Pain
The
Mind
May
Be
Force
Combined
Could
Take
Them
Afar
From
Us
Our
Growth
Is
Truncated
For
Their
Acts
Our
Shrines
Are
Made
Sacrilege
For
Their
Mess
May
We
Take
This
Route
To
Freedom

Physical Game (Escape Route Two)

('Violence in order to change an intolerable, unjust
Social order is not savagery: it purifies man.
Violence to protect and preserve an unjust, oppressive
Social order is criminal, and diminishes man.')
--- *Ngugi wa Thiong'o.*

My people
Who talk
Unwittingly about
the potholes
Of war
Have not
Seen an
Hue of
Peace brought
By the
Earth-shattering, cyclonic
Bursts of
Shells, tornado –
Of resilience

One of
The dangers
Of passivity
Is that
It never
Chokes oppression.
Danger number
Two is
It elongates
Day of
Reckoning, sweepstakes.
Another side
Of it

Is that
It forever
Holds man
Down, low…

Intellectual Capital (Escape Route Three)

('For wisdom is more precious than Rubies')
--- *Proverbs*, 8:11.
("I am a man of ideas, even in life or
In death, these ideas will live")
--- *Ken Saro-Wiwa.*

Brain titillated by sublime season -
Of a rising, path-finding sun,
That repackages far-flung ideas,
Is the tonic
for this ever changing tides of human creation.
It is the ointment for our sprained ankles:
Its balmy, soothing sensation, relaxes our frayed temper, being
        and minds that
Were left in the lurch by other competitors
In the marketplace of ideas, technology, materiality...

America, Europe –
The West barged into you, they found light –
That was all that Solomon asked:
His nest was full of eggs of epoch –
That hatched human civilization,
From whence, humanity knew another dimension of human
        capital!
We shall seek you first,
That's all we need in this journey.
You're the key to the doors of nature's bounties!

You do not fight with bare hand, not with brute force,
But your results of war are catholic:
Ocular images of where you're used,
Bring men closer to their Creator (they know more):
You're our unfettered Prometheus.
Arise from material slumber;

Carry the breastplate of wisdom.
With archly, measured steps, we would erect bridges
Over the gulf between poverty and creation's largess:
The archipelagos will be filled with the sands of time,
We will be blessed with technological wonders!

Our Power In Escrow

Our power has been exported,
Creating jobs for their people;
Our own will emerge to fight for our gifts,
It's only in escrow!
We're recreating our capital
To be knowledge based for this mental fight;
Our energies are only in the escrow!

The brume will fade away
Shattering the foothill of our yester years;
Springing us to the mountain of our worth.
The iron is on the fire,
We need to hammer while it's hot;
Or endlessly be endangered by their ruse.
Our power is only in escrow!

Our steel rolling mills run for human capital,
Our refineries hanker after our own professionals,
Not theirs, which keeps us low:
But ours, for us by us.
Bring back that capital
Lost in fight to them
While our earth burnt; we're no more on fire;
Our rebuilding power is only in escrow!

Earth Terrorists

They have nothing to give us, but hoopla,
They have nothing to offer, but somatic harm.
These terrorists hand out nothing, but ochre-coloured water,
While we can give ourselves pure one.
They chow down our earth with the ferocity of a lightning;
The earth in anguish for their deeds.
Drum and flute celebrate thuds of wardens in earth-crushing
           boots;
They march, while we squirm on the floor of the prison
As they whip our powerless bodies, crushing our teeth, blinding
           our eyes.
Snake are served as we asked for fish; they serve stone instead
           of bread.
The cell does justice to this decrepit zone,
Where we're packed like sardines,
The smell we produce races to heaven.
Some of us handcuffed in the streets -
Some killed by the justice of their kangaroo courts:
Our cries have reached the ends of the earth.

They use Land Use Decree
To sustain their exploitation,
The presidential fiat scaffolds their operations,
A panoply of naked terrorism -
Our earth is in peril:
The natural green canopy has given way
For a mushroom cloud -
Endorsing their mandate!
Iroko, *afara*, *abura*, mahogany…
In disarray for their acts;
Sluts at the waterfronts celebrate their bounding duty;
Local urchins in their large numbers call forth their mission;

The destroyed sea life tells their story -
What more signs fort their terrorism!
Our minds have been reconfigured
From their terrorism;
Our bodies inflicted with scares
From their violence;
Hope gone awry for their game plan.

Nihilists Of The Delta

We're from behind the barbed wires,
From choking landscape -
From whence angst, pain, brutality howled
Can't be believed to bring change.
Their heads are buried in the sands as the change comes.
They never read the signs on the wall;
Like Thomas, they want to dip their evil finger into the wound
      of time
To be sure we could upturn our 'fate'.
When they do,
It will be a well; not a hole
For they doubted our resolve to fold this carpet of disservice.
Like the ostrich, their heads are religiously buried in the sands
      of change,
That will sweep them away into the sea.
They're laughing at our resolve,
Underestimating the powers of the disgruntled.
History must remind them of the pith of such people!
Let our action blow them away…
To oblivion, it must be!
May their heads in the grounds suffer illusion,
No vision for the blind,
Whose head is in the ground:
Let the oil blind them,
So we strike from all corners
From whence they've been raping our innocent earth, our
      trove.
What a sacrilege our gods must soon visit!

The Selects Of The Nation

We're the select of the nation,
Cut out for victimization.
We're the chosen of the land,
Naturally made to attract enemies.
We have never seen tender moment in our time,
We have been eyewitnesses to all kaleidoscope of human
        cruelty.
Dozens of fiats have been churned out for this act.

We're the chosen few,
Made to carry the albatross for all.
Our nature chains us:
An unsolicited load we carry!
What needless pain we bear for our nature,
Recreate us next time around
For we're chosen for a meltdown;
Not that we're preferred!

Vernal Breeze

1.
A fresh new breeze is blowing from all cusps,
An earth refreshed by peace is coming to stay;
Its inhabitants unfettered, unhitched
From Ogoni agonies, from ethnic cleansing:
In their hearts, on their lips,
We behold an era in retreat, bowing to the silent spring:
Its old ideas and practices
Being blown away like leaves from a motionless tree;
Its men washed ashore as the polluted waters drown them.
Silent spring is raining on the land
… rivers, creeks, estuaries knew aquatic destruction,
(before);
Brooks are springing to quench our thirst
After our tongue hankered after fresh water
Made undrinkable, ochre-coloured,
From their ecological genocide.
The silent spring is glued to the axletree,
Inseparably hooked to the wheels of change –
Harvesting lissom leaves, limber trees, lithe flower…

2.
A new order is sojourning to dwell among us,
Its freeing vibration could be felt from all bearings:
A system washing away the numbing waves that razed our earth
Will be its pillars:
Democratic patterns its motto.
Never again in the green world,
Would such calamity find anchorage:
The breeze of change will blow it down whenever it rises again.
Blow with incendiary fire:
Levelling the remnant structures they left to do mayhem again.
Let our shores be filled with their flotsam, all dead, putrid,
Trading places with the aquatics they destroyed!

A Letter From The Green World

Dear men of exploration,
Explore less
For I'm almost sapped of my contents:
Perennial sapping has made me weak,
Endless brutality has mangled my greens,
Interminable violence has affrayed my energies!
Mangy farm yields with back bent
From your activities are pointers to this destruction;
Charred space, a ghost of my former self,
Tells the exploitative story of the multinationals & our 'leaders'!
Dear men of red,
'Re-green' my world
by quitting my space.
This is all the green campaign coming from me
In this time of my environmental politics!

The Earth Superbugs

Their bodies are resistant to deliberations,
All peace talks have yielded no results,
Except more headache, more showdown.
It's better to engage in prophylaxis
Than treatment,
For when it settles in,
It never goes away:
They mutate -
Changing from one evil to the other,
All to make the parley insensate.

The Oputa Panel could not bring them to books;
The untouchables of the pack
Never listened to the "ranting" of this great commission
For they are foolproof, untouchable,
From the arrangement of the system they created for
        themselves by themselves.
All the justice commissions have cut no ice on them;
They rather reinforce their idea of new ploy:
The changing mask of the predator.

How do we tame their excesses, at least,
For the season resonates with their intractableness!
When shall they be caged, at last?
Before we're extinguished?
These men keep changing like the season;
Their vices change to suit the present order -
Changing men of the season,
The real superbug.
Environmental chameleons -
Your feint is a quicksand:
Sinking the weak in struggle for justice for our earth.

Why do they call you superbug?
Is it because you spurn medicine?
Delta nation is on the drawing board for you
Just for you, our earth is in ruins.
Borrow a leaf from history
Before you're run into the ground.
Like all diseases in history,
We shall have a cure for you soon,
No time wasting as it used to
For we're out to find a cure for you this time.

On Men & Oil

The best of a nation,
Is what is found in their heart;
Not in what they say;
Not in how they look,
For these are smokescreens,
Hiding their actual worldview.

The best of any nation,
Is deposited in their men,
Not in how they deal with other men,
Not in the way they profess sovereignty:
For these items are daubed with blasphemy,
Lurking their true colours

It's on the inside
That you find the real colour of a nation -
Stating beyond rhetoric
The reason for being;
Not in fireworks, not in diplomacy -
But on the inside
You find the best of a people.

It's in oil talk
That you know the best of a nation -
It's the reason for the entire national, global tempest.
The ability to swim against the tide
On this issue,
Stands a nation out:
That's where its best is located.

Nature's Unfinished Project

You deprived us of strength
To curb the vermin's greed,
You foreclosed us from meeting these gluttons on equal terms:
You nature,
You leave off projects
To be finished off by us for us –
Our complementing your task
Will not elude us,
For we're ready this time for this change of gear!
Your works are fragmentary –
All like a dog's breakfast,
You have left your job
For us to complete.

Special Fight

It's a different kind of fight:
In the war,
Many casualties recorded;
The crack of whips, brandishing of swords
And sparkling rapiers, lethal bludgeons
Lead us to an embattled kingdom:
The road to it,
Cluttered with the fallen,
The greats among them hanged.
The bodies beyond numerical assessment –
Because most are dead in their spirit, minds;
The portals, not without bodies littered before it.

It's a special war:
In the fight,
Shame to the gate of blood;
Not us (as they always imagined).
This war mirrors the strength of the ants!
They build structures with bare hands,
They use wisdom when danger looms,
They fight with fire in their bellies.
This war is not the ordinary -
That we all know, and expect.

It's an unusual fight:
In the battle,
The minions of the godfathers
Are in defeat;
The powers of their masters have failed them.
It's not the familiar ones –
Predictable, 'riggable', stoppable, 'lootable':
This warfare is the unusual:
A lesson for all the piers of this omnibus.

Changing Guard In The Delta

Our barns are filled with new possibilities
To overtake the robbers
Taking our possessions by sheer brute force.
Ogoniland is a cesspit of yester years's glory –
Land of decay, crumbling to injustice, going up in smoke.
Every ley line,
Separates us from yester year's image;
Each multinational fiendish activity,
Takes us further away from our blessings;
All planned attacks, mien
Diminish our inheritance.
All the ley lines leave a landmark:
A region in ashes –
The hyraxes have disappeared,
The squirrels have evaporated:
I can't sight the lions
Roaring in their kingdom, our great forests!
Our children can't see the sharks causing ripples in the deep
        seas;
The reapers' baskets are hungry for harvest;
The hunter has returned home with his pouch empty.
Let us fill our baskets with possibilities,
Driving away fear, pains ...
Gravitating strongly towards healing our land.
Let us change the guards –
Let new oil run the engine of our modern history
We have got to rid ourselves of this fawning mentality,
Forever pushing us to the fringe,
Leaving us potentially poisoned by our choices.
Let us change this overthrowing transition -
A patchwork of governance,
Replacing the sludge

With new oil:
The oil gluttons with men of honour.
Let the new broom sweep all muddle away,
And call forth our renaissance
Which has been on a cliff-hanger,
For their raid.
Change these gathering of loots
From our parliaments –
Sauntering dazed on roguish pathway of legislation.
Change the guard for renewed purpose,
That we may once again
Have true vision in our land:
Change this assembly of maids of dishonour
With men of honour.
Change this guard for the healing of the delta.
Our heirlooms are starved of stocks
For their ignorance in the house.
Change the lawmakers
Who change our lore
To work for their bellies
… and their masters'…
Change the sentry for they're drunk
From power – all men's bane.
Change the guard
For our airbags need fresh breeze –
Blowing away ides of stasis.

Delta, The Ground Zero

They have put you into the ground
Lifting themselves with your largess;
in the ground,
Your worth is sunk.
From graves,
Festooned with gravitas of our ancestors,
Dug with pride
– And awash with our lore,
Our ancestors wail;
Their graves and tombstones
Convulse
From the earthquake the explorers caused
To our earth.
Our earth is on ground zero;
The Twin Towers incident,
A mere child's play to this convulsion –
Leave all the green leaves
That form green canopy
Yellow, all tumbling down;
The carriers of these green canopy,
All sinking into the ground.
The earth made
Soft, all a quicksand;
Nothing to be sighted from all corners.
Your breasts are flabby
From the greed of the capitalists;
Your blood all sucked by white elephants;
Your brain unworkable
From their design.
The milk from your breast
Feeds the whole world –
That's why they all come to have a piece of your cake,

73

Running you aground!
They call you ground zero
That's your title;
Wake up before they call you "ground minus"!

The New Leviathans, The Multinationals

Who can make a pet of them?
Like a bird?
Or put them on a leash for our fragile economy?
Who can pull them in with a fishhook?
Who can fill their hide with harpoons?
Or seal their gaping mouth with a rope?
Crushing them has caused ripples,
Their sight is overpowering:
They hanker after the black gold, an aphrodisiac
… The ultimate lodestar, a flambeau unto their mission.

Their breath releases flashes of fire,
Their nostrils give out chimneys,
Their eyes send forth thunderous lightning,
Their hands, feet throw nations into vortex -
On their chest is written the byword:
Zero-sum game in global operation,
The bane of our snail-paced growth, our meltdown!

They don't shy away from our swords;
They don't see strength in our potentials;
They don't respect our environment;
They rape it every step of the way!
Their strength is lodged in their technological depth,
A mutative crag their forte:
They clutter our earth with their pipes,
… With our blood…

Acid Rain

Your scalding pouring
With virulent torrents
Burns my earth to bits -
Crushes my earth to pieces;
Your polluted contents by their genius
Deepen the footprints of ecological swoop.

You have made our soil barren
Your corrosive, acidic wand
Has plucked out our inheritance:
Our world has disappeared!

Your exploitative presence
With ghoulish fever
Freezes our economy,
It kills our marine means.

Oil, The Growing Planet Terror

All great
And small nations on earth
Thrive on you;
All the birds of the air
And the hungry
Nestle in your bough;
All superpowers
And small nations
Oil the wheels of their economic engines on you!
The superpowers hurl fire
Because of you;
They slaughter humankinds, the powerless
But for you;
They war against the defenceless
For your sake;
In search of you,
Small nations go hungry,
In pursuit of the means you bring,
"tiny" states carry the albatross.
Our earth never sleeps
As they overheat you
– global warming!
Our space never closes its eyes
As they rob you nakedly.

All nations
Live under your shade;
The masters of the universe
routinely
Dialogue to annihilate you;
The rulers of the earth

seasonally
Gather to arrest your development;
They
perennially
Invest in ideas, arms, and technology to clone you!

All nations quake whenever you're scarce,
All streams on earth cannot trade places with your value:
Their camels graze on arid fields when you're off the stage;
Their industries run amok when you're missing in action;
They call us fault line states to act their script:
Our earth is branded "warring region" to remove our green
canopy.

... Like a woman in labour,
Our pain grows every inch towards giving birth.
They have dug trenches to arrest our escape,
They have put up moat to cage us!
...With full neo-colonialist hardware,
They have descended on our planet to deepen our pain:
With new killing method,
Their approach towers on high,
It's overshadowing our planet with its branches,
Stretching to all corners of our earth.

Printed in the United States
By Bookmasters